THE TULIP-FLAME

Cleveland State University Poetry Center

New Poetry
Frank Giampietro, Series Editor
Michael Dumanis, Founding Series Editor

For a complete listing of titles please visit
www.csuohio.edu/poetrycenter

The Tulip-Flame

CHLOE HONUM

Cleveland State University Poetry Center
Cleveland, Ohio

LIBRARY OF CONGRESS CATALOGING-IN-PUBLICATION DATA

Honum, Chloe, 1981–

[Poems. Selections]

The Tulip-Flame / Chloe Honum.—First edition.

  pages cm.—(New Poetry)

Includes bibliographical references and index.

ISBN 978-0-9860257-5-4 (paperback : acid-free paper)

I. Title.

PS3608.O555A6 2014

811'.6—dc23

2013045986

5 4 3 2   FIRST EDITION

This book is published by the Cleveland State University Poetry Center,
2121 Euclid Avenue, Cleveland, Ohio 44115-2214
www.csuohio.edu/poetrycenter and is distributed by
SPD / Small Press Distribution, Inc. www.spdbooks.org.

Cover art: Bust (Impression), life size: 17" × 21.5" × 13", 2005, cast glass,
© 2005 Karen LaMonte

Cover photo: Martin Polak
Author photo: Victoria Marie Bee
Book design: VJB/Scribe

ACKNOWLEDGMENTS

I would like to thank the editors of the following publications, in which these poems, sometimes in different forms, first appeared.

The Adroit Journal: "Alone with Mother"

AGNI: "Come Back"

Bat City Review: "June in Arkansas" and "Revenant"

Bellingham Review: "Ballerina, Released" and "Spring II"

The Economy: "Bright Death" and "Hunt"

The Journal: "Ballerina in Winter," "December," and "Nursing Home"

Linebreak: "Evening News"

Memorious: "Crossing the Three-Rope Bridge," "Danse des Petits Cynges," and "Thirteen"

The Missouri Review Online: "My Great Aunt Billie at Ninety-Two"

Nimrod International Journal: "Directing the Happy Times," "Last of the Ballerina I Was," and "Silence Is a Mother Tongue"

Orion: "Assembling Faith"

The Paris American: "Ballerina at Dawn" and "To the Anorexic"

The Paris Review: "Fever"

Plume: "January in West Texas"

Poetry: "Dress Rehearsal" and "Spring"

Shenandoah: "The Tulip-Flame"

The Southern Review: "Dressing Room," "Leaving the Hospital," "Leaving Town" (as "Dusk"), "Seated Dancer in Profile," and "Visiting Hours"

Thrush: "Hours"

"Crossing the Three-Rope Bridge" also appeared in *Best of the Net 2012*, edited by Marilyn Kallet (Sundress Publications, 2012).

"Spring" also appeared in *Best New Poets 2010*, edited by Claudia Emerson (Samovar Press, 2010).

"Directing the Happy Times" also appeared in *Best New Poets 2008*, edited by Mark Strand (Samovar Press, 2008).

I would also like to thank the following individuals and institutions whose support made this book possible:

Cleveland State University Poetry Center, the Djerassi Resident Artists Program, the Kerouac Project of Orlando, the MacDowell Colony, the New York State Summer Writers Institute, the Poetry Foundation, the Sewanee Writers' Conference, and Summer Literary Seminars-Russia.

Sarah Lawrence College, Texas Tech University, and the University of Arkansas.

Curtis Bauer, Geoffrey Brock, Dennis Covington, Michael Heffernan, Marie Howe, Rebecca Gayle Howell, Jacqueline Kolosov, Mary La Chapelle, Thomas Lux, Davis McCombs, Meaghan Mulholland, John Poch, Michael Shewmaker, Ron Slate, Ariadne Thompson, and William Wenthe.

I am deeply grateful to Frank Giampietro for his careful editing and to Tracy K. Smith for selecting the book.

Thank you to my family, Alaine Booth and Stefan Honum.

And to Jacob Shores-Arguello, for love and laughter.

For my grandmother
Elaine Anderson

CONTENTS

Birds are never just birds in Chloe Honum's debut collection, *The Tulip-Flame*. Perhaps that is true to a certain extent in any poem, where gazing out at the world provides the poet with an opportunity to see and describe what is known or felt just as much as what is seen. But here, in these poems Honum has fashioned through the lens of stark and ongoing loss, it is even truer. Here, Honum is urging the world to do an even more active, more searing kind of double duty. Birds are not merely birds, but members of a jury that sit beyond and above the landscape, determining what will prevail. Elsewhere, a crow, the offspring of Stevens's blackbird, hovers, turning over the speaker's actions in its "sky-knowing mind." Or they are flying past, "like white scarves in wind," elegant and fleeting as a woman's brief life.

Even the flowers invoked by the collection's title are perceived through the shock of the collection's central and ongoing loss —namely the death of the speaker's mother, "as was her plan." The tulips startle a landscape awake, and urge into feeling the reader who encounters them. But, fixed in place and rooted to the ground, the flower's shock of color and commotion mostly announces the failure of anything, anything at all to "have intervened." Everything at Honum's command—the birds and the flowers and even the body itself—is expertly seen, exquisitely signaling.

Honum's speaker—perhaps Honum herself—was at one point a ballerina. And we see the ballet master, the black or white or red tutus, the grand jetés. There is evidence of the dancer's life—a life governed by poise, by rigor, and by a particular obsession with beauty—in many poems across the collection. These things appear, quite often, as themselves, as elements of a milieu. But the manner in which dance mostly lives in the poems, even the poems that have nothing ostensibly to do with the ballet, is in their sense of having been expertly choreographed: in their blocking or staging, in the ways that people and things move within their lines. These are poems that teach us not only to see that which is visible, but to re-envision movement, to perceive feeling as action, as "the sound of light // falling. The gray sky pinning / a single planet in its hair."

I am so very taken by the exquisite power and grace in every single one of these poems, so arresting in their honesty and in their unflinching ability to scour the world for image after indelible image. Like a dancer, or like a dance, *The Tulip-Flame* is expertly wrought, built upon muscle and instinct and crafted into something that feels inevitable and spontaneous. To me, these poems are driving toward what all truly great poems set their sights upon: an encounter with the real; an instant, even fleeting, where speaker and poet and reader converge at the feet of something large and necessary. Not merely skill, or intelligence, or that which is beautiful. But the terrible force and delicate balance that enable love, loss, joy, and grief to fly through our lives.

Tracy K. Smith
October 2013
Brooklyn, New York

THE TULIP-FLAME

Love, love, my season.
Sylvia Plath

I

SEATED DANCER IN PROFILE

Spring

Mother tried to take her life.
The icicles thawed.
The house, a wet coat
we couldn't put back on.

Still, the garden quickened,
the fields were firm.
Birds flew from the woods'
fingertips. Among the petals

and sticks and browning fruit,
we sat in the grass and
bickered, chained daisies, prayed.
All that falls is caught. Unless

it doesn't stop, like moonlight,
which has no pace to speak of,
falling through the cedar limbs,
falling through the rock.

Ballerina in Winter

Through this season given to storms, I wake at dawn to practice. I drag aside the living room chairs, like heavy dreams, and play softly a tape of ballet music. Sometimes I go outside to work on grand jetés, to run barefoot and push off from wet concrete while Mother and Sister sleep. They know that I am changing but not how quick. Sometimes the sky is violet above a jury of silver birds. Sometimes mist. Sometimes lightning slices the hills straight through and doesn't hit a nerve.

Dress Rehearsal

Branches etch the film of ice
on the studio window. A crow looks in,
hopping and shrieking when I dance
in my black tutu trimmed with silver.

The ballet master says, *You are its mother.*
But in a crow's sky-knowing mind
could I be so misconstrued?
Out of the blackest

cold-wet air, the crow seems molded.
The stars will not wake up to guide it
back to the creek of shadows
where it was formed. Practice, practice.

I am smoke in darkness, climbing away
from a burning hut in an otherwise empty field
on which the fire is slight and low,
and the rest of it is snow.

Hunt

Every year my sister and I
sifted through the clutter
of early spring,

of what the warm earth
coughed up: fresh death,
nothing wasted.

Out of the light's loose skin
trumpet-flowers formed.
How still they were,

those pale gold mornings
with Mother sleeping.
How we'd glide from

the house to the garden,
like a pair of falcons
toward a rustle in the grass.

Visiting Hours

The summer before, Mother wrote *Cum Deo* in permanent marker all around our house, on lampshades, picture frames, and vases. Sitting on the edge of her hospital bed, I spoke in whispers yet my voice had never been so loud. Because I asked her to, she said she wanted to live—promised she was happy she hadn't died. Birds flew by like white scarves in wind. I was fourteen, a trembling ballerina, a stone. My love was a knife against her throat.

Seated Dancer in Profile

after Degas

The dancer sits on the ground. She wears a dress with a low back and a bow at the waist. She is surrounded by blue, and her hand touches the nape of her neck. It is up to you what this gesture means. She looks away—first from the painter and then the world. To love her is to accept that she will never turn around.

Assembling Faith

A huge turkey came
down the path. Serene,
only slightly more

beautiful than ugly.
It looked as though
it had made itself

out of morning's spare parts.
I wanted to put something
together like that,

without a mirror.
Long feathers.
Waxy, red dribble—

and yet it glided
almost regally
into the misty woods.

II

ALONE WITH MOTHER

Thirteen

The trees wrote their last scarlet notes.
[*shame*]
Silence grew inside me. By winter
my voice felt like a bowl
of very still water; [→ *silent*]

for hours at a time nothing moved it.
Here is the house; a table
beneath a golden light,
Mother's closed bedroom door,

a window. Here is the garden.
She wanted to move away
from us, I knew,
and I'd have let her. *Go,*

I whispered, but alone,
while watching a sparrow [→ *protection and joy*]
splash in a basin:
emerald water, spindly leaves, feathers.
[*bright green*]   [*Long*]

17

Danse des Petits Cygnes

Famous dance from Swan Lake

When there's a song in my head
where God should be,
I yearn for the ballet master,

(crave/desire)

for winters

at the studio where I
was one of four cygnets. → *young swan*
Rehearsals ran late.
Night swayed on its green stem → *plant*

swing / move slowly

and I couldn't comprehend
we'd ever be clipped from it. → *shorten/cut*
Even seeing us together
in our white tutus—

like roses standing naked
on a coffin—I was soothed
by the sound of rain
hissing through the leaves.

making a sound

Alone with Mother

We came out of the sea at dusk
and walked through the dune grass.
Like runaways, we were free

→ talk rapidly

of the house and its babble:
pill bottle labels, shopping lists.
The ocean banged and frothed. *→ fizz/foam*

In the car, we sat a long time,
the keys a silver
starfish in her lap, silence

a kind of love between us.

Nursing Home

My mother takes me to meet you for the first and only time.
We find you in a chair in the garden. You call my mother Alan,
her oldest brother's name, and she laughs sadly. *I know about
you*, I want to say. *Mean drunk. Molester.* I am seven or eight. It
is fall, the Zen season, the trees clearing their minds. Golden sap.
Lavender. Grandfather, where is your memory? I would like to
help you look for it. I would like to see you crawl under the shrubs.

*ashamed
very low stells*

Ballerina at Dawn

By then I'd learned
a triple pirouette, [→ spin / twirl]
which felt like disappearing.

[cloud ↑]
At dawn, mist widened
the space between the trees.
I walked toward the studio,

[river]
past the creek and its pale-
veined stones. Sunlight
measured the icicles. [→ ice]

And for a moment,
passing beneath those
swords of slow rain,

I heard the birds lift
their hunger-song
from early to midwinter.

[winter can be a
harsh season for
birds]

To the Anorexic

Sleepy child, what are you sewing? Where do you imagine you will wear it? Morning falls like yards of satin in your lap. Each time Mother wraps her arms around you, your shoulders are smaller than she expects—do you enjoy this, that it takes a moment to find you? It is winter and the fields are numb. Then it's spring and poppies flaunt their blood-soaked composure. For months you've felt the tug of hunger, like a balloon tied to your wrist. The sky asks nothing. Let your hand float up, and answer.

Leaving the Hospital

The nurses said our mother,
who had tried to die,
would be all right and could
come home tomorrow.

Flowers wilted in their glass fists.
Alone in the elevator
my sister was sad
and I was angry,

but turning to face her
was like turning to face
my heart. And the words
we spoke, what were they,

walking out amid the soft
groans of winter?
Wet grass, afterlight
streaming through the clouds.

The Tulip-Flame

My sister's painting this: a hill, a lane
that winds around the hill, and a wide field
of tulips with a centered tulip-flame.

She rolls her brush through gray and adds the rain
in tiny flicks, glinting arrows of cold.
My sister's painting this: a hill, a lane.

Last year our mother died, as was her plan.
It's simpler to imagine something could
have intervened. The centered tulip-flame → *cheerful thoughts*

startles the scene; the surrounding ones are plain
pastels, while this one's lit with a crimson fold.
My sister's painting this: a hill, a lane

of cobblestones, a watery terrain
of dripping flowers. Her strokes, elsewhere controlled,
flare out and fray around the tulip-flame

as if it were an accident, a stain,
a blaze in the midpoint of a wet field.
My sister's painting this: a hill, a lane,
a tulip field, and one astounding flame.

Spring II

Sister, it is a beautiful afternoon
and I am stuck in an evening
of soundless lightning.

mimic/copy

I want to emulate the roots
loosening their white grips,
to feel sunlight on my knuckles.

Almost before my eyes, spring
spits daffodils on the lawn.
Still, I stand stiffly,

flowers

remembering Mother, her slim
form alone at the end of the garden,
the fruit trees newly in bloom

and how I, frightened or jealous
of their song, would call and call
without a thing to tell her.

Snow White

Queen, you were ~~starlight~~
obsessing over an empty cradle,
then over the door to the cradle room,
then over the hallway to the door.

I too feel my life is moving backward.
I spend hours recalling
how I ~~reeled~~, as if from dream
to dream, when you knocked,

how ~~crows~~ swooped and dived
like black fire behind you.
The prince tells me I moan
for you in my sleep—

good star, bad mother, lone tree
in a vast field on which the seasons hang
their sheets, wet and colored
with all the illnesses of beauty.

Ballerina, Released

On stage each night I shape a single story.
It's later, driving home, that vertigo
sets in. I lose all focus, see the roads
tangling in the wind. Rain sings on stones
that lead to my front door; its music holds
no cues for me. I light a cigarette
and lean against a tree. Clear blossoms froth
along the boughs, a daddy longlegs prowls
over the grass, its legs on eight blade tips.
The moon is spinning in a sack of mist.
How can I sleep? I dance the murders of
the Firebird, my red tutu a flame
in a cave, then fall. I cannot grasp my life.
I float. The garden shakes behind my smoke.

Directing the Happy Times

Think April, late, when all things tilt, quiver
with color and rain. Begin, hibiscus, drip

like a woman in wet clothes. With deeper curve,
magnolia, you ache and brown. Last drop,

knock down the honeybee; on three, it bobs,
a cork in water, that's its time to shine.

Wisteria, study the air where it throbs.
Be amethyst. Focus. I'll need the vine

to fully engage the tree, lilies to white
one by one as Mother walks the lane.

It must be this precise, or, simply put,
she'll get distracted, fail to read her line;

she will not laugh, the waiting stagehands' cue.
Lights down. Enter the shadows who carry you.

III
FEVER

Hours

I stood gazing at the hills—
water, smoke, clouds—
going over how I'd failed
to make him love me.

I did this for hours.
Then, touching the soft
earlike folds of mushrooms,
switched to *How alone I am,*

how lovely. Night fell.
Stars woke above the trees.
All the way back home
I strolled until, on the porch,

a large moth collided
with my throat and shuddered
there, as if attached to me,
trapped in a wheel of air.

Sixteen

Shoulder deep in the lake at dusk, fish slid
like flaps of light by my legs, my hair swished behind me.
The world was of small noise that summer,
avoiding words, slipping past mirrors.

I sat on the dock, my skin wet and shimmering,
watching birds glide in their flat S for the instant
they swooped, as if something uttered
swung them around by their beaks,

and the invisible ribbon of their pattern
pulled, like a bow, untied. (In a letter
he wrote, *Je t'aimais, Je t'aime, Je t'aimerai.*)
Some said I was dewy-eyed, walking home

from the lake in my towel, studying fireflies,
with their fairylike name and blinking charm.
But what about the moment they come on,
when the dark meets their skill and they crawl to the tips of the reeds?

The Good Kind

As the summer rain
eases off, insects begin

to buzz and leap,
to crawl in and out

of the flowers. I hope,
wherever you are, you don't

dislike your memories of me.
Our hands were so young.

The hurt we'd cause
was always there, waiting

like death—the good kind.
And didn't we hear it

while making love
in the steamy grass:

birdsong, as it sounded
in the minds of the trees.

Evening

I want to try to tell you
about remorse, but I've grown
fond of silence, how it sits
beside me like a pet.

[On the porch a crow begins
to interrogate nightfall,
as if its eyes will not adjust.
A neighbor boy

opens his bedroom window
and allows to wander,
at the end of his flashlight,
a golden moon. Now the wind

won't let the leaves alone—
they swirl against my door
like words to a sentence,
out of order and burning.

My Great Aunt Billie at Ninety-Two

New Zealand

How often did she think of him,
the American soldier
who said that he'd return
and they would marry?

Did he already have a wife?
Did he die? Did the days
feel like wave after wave
of silence? She was a chorus girl.

We were out walking.
On the ground were tiny
birds, like wet handkerchiefs.
I was the girl who came back,

she said, *as the curtain lowered,*
and with a little hop
she blew to the woods—
the river, the birds—a kiss.

Fever

Alone, which has grown to mean *without you,*
    I sweat in our old bed. In the bay, the storm's orchestra tunes.
Thunder, and my next expression is one of yours.
    As if in need of something lost, wind tears
through the garden. It checks all my blooms. Rain
    falls in curtains from the roof of the porch, a thin
gap where arms could part them, hems of clattering hail.
    Foghorns tunnel through salty haze, the full-
of-vapor sound of a vanished horizon, roaming and slow.
    Like a conductor's elbows, the wings of a crow
rise tip to tip and hover in the naked readiness that spreads
    from the sea, through swirling reeds, to the bed
where I ache and roll. The lilac light falls suddenly dim.
    Blinking through sweat, I imagine: you've just left and will come
back for me soon, a bouquet of ice in your arms.

December

I have learned that to be in shock is a kind of mercy. I stayed there a long time. One winter, I was a preschool teacher. At recess, the children would pick things up and bring them to me as gifts. A pebble, a piece of bark, a dirty feather. Often a child would say, *I got this for you.* As in I have come back from a journey. As in I remembered. I learned the question *who wants a story* is always welcome. The days were short. It was snowing.

Leaving Town

A few hard flakes of snow
drift along the empty highway.
I am slow to remember

your voice, my pretty mother.
Though I feel you with me
(as gentle and focused as a finger

moving across a map),
the wind in the leafless trees
makes a raw sound. And where

does he go, that shadowy figure
who handles my memories?
Sometimes, if I wait, I see him

in blue winter dusk
loading another wagon of stars
and hitching it to his old mule.

IV

DUSK

Crossing the Three-Rope Bridge

Today it stormed. The clouds were flame-base blue
and smoldered close to the treetops. Lightning
double blinked. Ten years have passed, and not
Like that. By dusk the rain had ceased, the birds,
giddy with worm-lust, sang to the softened earth.
I tried to sleep but thought of the bridge at camp:
three ropes above a rushing creek, my turn
to cross, you on the far bank wringing your hands.
I walked, heel toe, heel toe—a fish, the gleam
on a rock below, its wound a swirl of red.
The world forgave your attempts, but I
held out. And when my foot slipped, the whole
sky gasped. You raised your hands as if to heaven.
The birds start up again. It's been forever.

One & Sadness
Anger
metaphores & describes how fast the time was passing

41

June in Arkansas

I gaze at moths, spiders, and horned beetles
    and recall pieces of my dreams: his voice here,
his hand there. Later I sweep the porch.
    Rivulets of sweat run down my throat and chest.
Who am I shining for? Phantom rain comes first,
    then real rain pours. Every day I weep.
Light returns: a silver haze, chaperoned by crows.
    I read for hours, sleep and wake. A string
of ants ties itself around my wrist. I wait
    to feel in my heart the moment when day turns
toward night, and the trees become like children
    walking home, asleep on their feet.

Revenant

The branches were all in slings
of mist when you came back.
You had left something behind.

As you searched,
the world was quiet; it ceased
clinking its spoon against

the bowl of morning.
I didn't know what it was
but I wanted to hide it,

the already hidden thing.
And I followed you through
the house and back out,

down to where the sun lit
a clump of cold, white flowers—
all that it would light that day.

Dressing Room

At the hospital morgue, I put on purple gloves, which made my hands look like fish beneath the surface of a pond. A man unzipped the bag so I could see my friend's face.

The dancers change into costume, stretch. A curling iron heats up on a table. Pairs of false eyelashes wait in their plastic kits. Around the edge of the mirror, a few light bulbs are always out, like the dim regions on a map.

It is natural to look for yourself first in a picture. To reassure yourself that you are there. The morgue was small and cold. The chemical smell made it suddenly hard to breathe. *You won't*, the ballet master said, when I asked what to do if I forgot.

Bay

Tonight, I listen to
the applause of small waves
and need you here. LOVE

stands on the bedside table
in majuscule letters. Branches
in a waterless vase hold out

their berries like pricked fingers.
Today, I stepped into a morgue
to see my dearest friend. I placed

my gloved hands on the plastic
over her cold hands. *Oh, God,*
oh, yes, I want to hear you say

as you push into my flesh,
deepen my heart, like pink light
above the ocean turning red.

Bright Death

I knew that it was true.
The sound of light

falling. The gray sky pinning
a single planet in its hair.

Days later, I lay in the grass
and woke to dusk, a moth

writing erasing writing
in quick, looping cursive.
A tattered scrap of a thing.
My voice. Its see-through wings.

[handwritten marginalia: "attach with a pin", "in poor condition", "a piece of something"]

46

Last of the Ballerina I Was

I can still hear
the violins
and feel her
last jeté, how *a dance*
the stage
rippled beneath her *waved/flows*
as dusk ripples
in the slipstream
of a bird
whose sudden
ascension *rise*
strands its
shadow
on the shore.

January in West Texas

Once, I preferred nights. How they arrived one tied to the next like silk scarves, knots of daylight between them. I frequented starry places. Now, I walk on parched grass. Dust lifts, swirls, and resettles. In a letter to his brother, Keats writes, *Our bodies every seven years are completely fresh-material'd … 'Tis an uneasy thought that in seven years the same hands cannot greet each other again.* Most afternoons I lie down, sunlight streaming through the window, inviting sleep. I follow a rustling noise, like leaves falling, or a fortune-teller turning the pages of her newspaper to the obituaries.

Evening News

On the news, war tumbles on.
Protestors fall in the street.
A child comes home

to find her mother,
father, and babysitter dead.
A mother and baby

are diagnosed together.
A sophomore girl is gunned down,
by mistake, in an elevator.

I switch off the television
and step outside. What does it take
to see what darkness gives?

Tonight, it crosses my mind
how gone you are, and stars,
if stars say anything, say Otherwise.

Silence Is a Mother Tongue

Large birds push off from branches, heads down,
    their wings turning like oars. Beneath a net
of mosquitoes, a corner of the lake's filmy surface
    has thickened to a palette of lime, brown, and milky blue.
When she was well, my mother gardened—plush
    black irises, heavy orchids. What I have left
are the sustained gazes between us. By the playground
    a fish-shaped kite, snagged on a power line, sways.
Its clear fins shimmer. I remember the summer
    I overturned a muddy rock in the garden and found, like teeth
grown in quiet, a cluster of quartz crystal. I showed my mother
    in the kitchen. Blackbirds walked the clothesline;
their pencil-yellow beaks etched the stillness. Our silences
    were like this, something turned over, her eyes assessing it.

Come Back

I can't see all of any horse at once.
They weave through twilight, in and out of sight,
as the sky drains of color, enters dusk.

The barn's a bloodstain on an ivory dress,
lost in the skirt, a spiraling red kite.
I can't see all of any horse at once.

Between us there is only field and dust,
a fence and a shadow-fence. Beside me lightning
splashes the hillside, loosens it so dusk

can wring each soggy evergreen, unlace
pink threads of berries from the shrubs. I wait.
I can't see all of any horse at once.

The moon has flown and in its place a husk
clings to the sky. The horses figure eight
in single file. Through rain-sown drapes of dusk

I try to count them, climb up on the fence.
Their foreheads shine with pearly stars, ghost-lit.
I can't see all of any horse at once—
they multiply, and shiver in the dusk.

[Handwritten margin note, left: "repitition — ould be ntrued as why? or why he can't see the whole horse."]

[Handwritten note, bottom: "Not being able to see all the horse could show how she can no longer see all in life, without Pamela [NOTES]"]

NOTES

"Danse des Petits Cygnes": The title refers to a dance from *Swan Lake*, composed by Pyotr Ilyich Tchaikovsky.

"Ballerina, Released": *The Firebird* is a ballet composed by Igor Stravinsky.

"Bright Death" is for Elaine Anderson.

"Come Back" is for Pamela Honum.

ABOUT THE AUTHOR

Chloe Honum is the recipient of a 2009 Ruth Lilly Fellowship from the Poetry Foundation. Her poems have appeared in *The Paris Review*, *Poetry*, *The Southern Review*, and elsewhere. She has received fellowships from the MacDowell Colony, the Kerouac House of Orlando, and the Djerassi Resident Artists Program. Honum was born in Santa Monica, California, and was raised in Auckland, New Zealand.